FADING AWAY
WITH ALZHEIMERS

FADING AWAY
WITH ALZHEIMERS

A Caregiver's Story

Bill Gordon Smith

To order additional copies of this book, contact:
Xlibris Corporation
1-888-795-4274
www.Xlibris.com
Orders@Xlibris.com
39368

CONTENTS

To Pray

Do not pray for easy lives.
Pray to be stronger men.
Do not pray for tasks
equal to your powers.
Pray for powers equal
to your tasks.

—Anonymous

Note: The last line is important—remember that you are not Superman: If you need help—ask for it!

CHAPTER 1

My Story . . . So Far

The scriptures clearly proclaim that the Lord will not burden you with more than you can carry; many times during the past few years, I have questioned that. Sometimes it seems the load is so incredibly heavy that I wonder if anyone can carry *it*, but somehow, he does provide the strength required.

My story is real and it is ongoing. It is now 1991, ten years into the nightmare of Alzheimer's disease. It is not my intent to relate a story of self-pity; rather, my focus is intended to tell what has happened and continues to unfold with Jo, my wife of forty-three years. This dreadful disease has not only affected Jo, but also our two sons and me. We are still learning to deal with the relentless deterioration of Jo, and it continues to be tough on all of us. I am sure that if Jo could communicate what torment and frustration that she feels, our individual feelings would be pale in comparison. Her abilities to communicate, think, and reason are gone. It has been that way for almost five years. She is not unlike a little child; sometimes frightened, happy, angry, loving, and most often exhibiting a bewildered blank stare—all within the span of a few minutes.

Never in my wildest dreams did I realize the possibility of a tragedy such as this would ever surface in our lives, but it did. It struck like the proverbial bolt of lightning without warning. I say without warning because at the time, I did not view the little "incidents" happening in our life as anything serious. However, in retrospect, I will attempt to outline the beginning as it appeared to me. I have since reconstructed some of those little "incidents" that caused others and me to know something was happening to Jo.

Things were going horribly wrong, we had no idea what our future held. "Alzheimer's disease, what is it, is it serious, is there a treatment or a cure, what can we expect, what should we expect?" We asked those questions and dozens more; some of which we cannot fully answer, but only wonder about.

I have since learned (since the onset of this "thing"), you never know when Alzheimer's actually starts. But through reliving the early stages, one can develop a reasonably accurate blueprint of what happened, and when you think *it* happened.

Back in 1981, we did not know much about the disease; many of us had never heard of Alzheimer's. Once it dawned on me that something was wrong, I quickly became a self-imposed student in an attempt to educate myself on the disease. I wanted to read everything that I could get my hands on to try and learn whatever I could. Nothing, I repeat, nothing prepared our two sons and me for what was to ultimately develop in our lives.

I must stress as strongly and as accurately as I can, this book is not a clinically based handbook on Alzheimer's disease, dementia, senility, etc. It is intended to tell what has happened in my life as the surviving spouse and how I have attempted to cope with it. Hopefully, those faced with being a caregiver to an Alzheimer's victim can get some kind of insight on my experiences. I tried to help make our lives as smooth and orderly as possible. Maybe, just maybe, I can help others. I hope so.

CHAPTER 2

In the Beginning

How does one begin to tell about an ongoing nightmare? Carefully I suppose, because much of it may sound unbelievable to the listener, unless that listener or reader "has been there."

Every story has a beginning of course and ultimately, an ending. It is difficult to piece things together, particularly if it is deemed important to position the facts in proper sequence as they developed. By necessity and perhaps due to my own inability to recall accurate dates and meaningful time frames, my story may be somewhat disjointed, and at times, repetitive. There are valid reasons for this, which will be described later.

As for our "beginning," there are many dates that I do recall with bull's-eye accuracy. Jo and I met in January 1948. She was a sixteen-year-old senior in high school. I was nineteen, thought that I knew everything, and was prepared to attach the world and mold it to my own liking. Two months after she graduated from high school, at a more mature age of seventeen and I was twenty, we were married on July 26, 1948.

As we all remember, part of the traditional wedding vows stipulate that we take each other for better or worse, in sickness or in health, and like most young people on their wedding day, we had visions of everything being perfect—forever! Little did we realize what the future held for us.

Overall, I would have to say that it was good, full of caring, respect, love, and yes, heartache. The good times far out weighed the tough times; that is the way it should be. We had no idea what would so drastically alter our lives thirty-three years later. I took my marriage vows seriously. I have abided by them as best that I knew how, and I have no regrets.

We have two wonderful sons: Don, now forty, and Glen, age thirty-eight. They will be interwoven into this story as my thoughts evolve. I would be remiss if I failed to mention our three perfectly beautiful, intelligent, sweet, and wonderful granddaughters. Don't all grandparents talk like that? Heather, age eighteen, and Holly, age sixteen, belong to Don, and Stephanie, age six, is Glen's pride and joy. With that as a thumbnail sketch of our family, perhaps it will enable you to associate with some degree of continuity, who is who in my story.

When a person is stricken with certain kinds of disease, quite often it can be identified as having a starting point, or at least a relatively identifiable time frame. That is not so with Alzheimer's disease; one never knows when *it* starts.

CHAPTER 3

Thoughts and Ideas

I wish that we could identify that *someone* who gave us all these wise sayings, those thought-provoking quotes that we have heard over the years. There are two that I have always liked, which believe it or not, have helped me throughout my adult life and have helped me cope with the monumental hurdles normally associated with Alzheimer's. The first one is great! If we stop and think about it, it says a lot about all of us as human beings:

> Intelligent people talk about ideas, average people talk about things,
> small people talk about other people.

It is partially descriptive of Jo. She was a very bright girl—full of ideas. She would execute and apply her ideas; and if it did not work fairly and honestly to all concerned, she would develop an alternative to achieve a goal.

I am confident there is some degree of bias in my appraisal of Jo, but she was intelligent about so many things. Yes, she was average, too, because she talked about things. This trait undoubtedly stemmed from her abilities as an excellent nursery school (preschool) teacher. She had to talk about *things* with her kids. To do that, as a part of the teaching process, she obviously used her positive attitude and talent by injecting ideas. I am sure that her students learned from her techniques.

The last line, small people talk about other people, did *not* apply in her life; it had no place in her life! She often said (to me, as well as to our boys, Don and Glen), "If you can't say something good, positive, and constructive about others, don't say it." Wouldn't it be nice if the whole world could adopt a similar philosophy?

The other quote that I feel is so appropriate in this story and can cause us to *think* is this:

> Yesterday is a cancelled check, tomorrow is nothing more than a promissory note, today is the only day that is negotiable.

Quite a meaningful thought, but I must offer a qualifier for my overall interpretation of it's meaning. At least to me, without all of our yesterdays, we have no memories. Thank goodness that we do have memories. Granted, some are painful and difficult to replay in our minds, but, by far, I think most bring back the happy times and events in our lives. As for the tomorrows, I am glad for them. How else could we plan, prepare, and dream for happy times yet to materialize? Oh yes, I know, many will say, "Live one day at a time, today is the day that is negotiable, it is spendable." We can use it or we can waste it. If we use it wisely, it is destined to become a good memory; but if wasted, certainly it will become the *cancelled check*.

In Jo's case, it is so tragic and seemingly so unfair that she has been robbed of her yesterdays, todays, and tomorrows. Alzheimer's disease has committed the most horrible of crimes on her mind; it has destroyed her ability to think, reason, and communicate. The granddaughters have handled that fairly well, I guess. It has been particularly hard for Don to accept. Glen has viewed this in a reasonably healthy manner. Heather and Holly have literally grown up knowing that their "Oma" (a pet German name for grandmother) was ill. With Stephanie, I really do not know. As for me, I have cried a lot, but I am getting better.

By reconstructing times and events, I have concluded that early 1981 were the identifiable times when I knew something was wrong with Jo's behavior. Of course, I had no idea what it was or what lay in store for us, but it was clear that something was going haywire.

We were on one of our many travel experiences; thank God we had the opportunity and made those trips when we did, when I first realized that Jo was sick. We were on a trip to China in December 1980-January 1981. Her personality, which had always been one of fun and happiness, took on highly unusual characteristics. She cried for unknown reasons and became agitated and visibly angry. These incidents were for short periods, but completely out of character for her. Often, it seemed that she had little or no recollection of them the next day.

Upon our return from China, I contacted our family doctor and related my concerns about Jo. There were what seemed to be endless tests, evaluations, CAT scans, MRIs, and finally, that devastating interview with a neurologist. Several months before that interview, I felt that I had seen the handwriting on the wall. My doctor had subtly alluded to the possibility of Alzheimer's, but he wanted to be as sure as possible. He explained that the only way to clinically diagnose the disease was upon an autopsy—what a chilling thought! By this time, I had read so much material on the subject that I was prepared for what the neurologist was going to tell me, "Jo exhibited a textbook case of Alzheimer's."

I was so prepared, if you can call it that, I started making arrangements to retire from my job so that I could be home to take care of her. I retired in November 1983. My postretirement career was now that of a "caregiver." In my mind, I was good at it for about seven years.

CHAPTER 4

Early Years

During the early stages, Jo was still reasonably functional; that is, she could still talk with me, perform personal hygiene requirements, go to the bathroom, feed herself, etc. Other tasks seemed to give her a problem, such as cooking (which she always loved to do and was very proficient at it), dressing herself, driving, balancing the checkbook, and several other things.

Beginning in about mid-1984, it seemed the whole world was falling apart for both of us. Her abilities rapidly deteriorated. She became very disoriented, confused, and so frustrated. Stress was beginning to take its toll on me, and if that was not enough, I was diagnosed as having a pituitary brain tumor. Prior to that diagnosis, we had planned a trip to England where we would "live like a local" for a few months. I had already rented a house, made arrangement for a rental car, and had even bought plane tickets; all of which had to be cancelled. Looking back, I now think my tumor problem triggered a rapid decline in Jo's condition.

I had brain surgery in July 1984. That recovery period, plus caring for Jo, was difficult to say the least; and our problems seemed to compound. Her sleep patterns became severely disturbed, which obviously impacted my sleep. There were many, many nights of no sleep at all. Jo was constantly getting in and out of bed, wandering around the house crying and quite often yelling or making nonstop nonsensical chatter. She could not sleep, and I was learning to rest as best as I could, usually with one eye open.

One particularly bad night, I found by accident that she would become calmer by riding in a car. Frequently, we could be found cruising the freeways around the

Bay Area (California), often at three or four o'clock in the morning. Sometimes, we would stop at a restaurant for pie and coffee, but it proved to be not always the wise thing to do. She had a compulsion to "be on the move," and consequently, after ordering our early morning snack, she would become extremely restless and agitated. Many times, we left the pie and coffee untouched and started driving again. It may seem silly to others driving around like that, but it worked for me (us). I reached the point that I would do just about anything to quell the yelling, hitting, etc.

Everything that I had read and been told about Alzheimer's warned me about episodes of violence. I could not imagine Jo being like that since she had always been a docile, easygoing person. My views changed after several bites, bloody lips, and/or nosebleeds. She would often turn violent for no apparent reason; she was not the same sweet girl that I had known all these years.

I quickly realized the terrible things that I had read were coming into reality. This stage, the violent stage, went on from early April 1986 through May or June 1988. Often, she would telegraph her mood swings, which were wide and varied, by narrowing her eyes and lips. These clues taught me to be ready for almost anything; nevertheless, I still "caught it." I knew it was not Jo anymore. Her mind was rapidly deteriorating as well as her physical self. During this period, she literally refused to eat, resulting in a considerable weight loss. She dropped almost forty pounds in approximately seven months. She reached a low of eighty-eight pounds, yet in 1991 she weighed in at about 103 pounds. She was truly fading away.

Incidentally, starting in late 1983 I became a pretty good cook. I prepared all meals, did all grocery shopping, laundry, ironing, and housecleaning; those things that Jo had done for so many years. She did them so well, but now she could not; she did not remember how. Memory loss was becoming very pronounced. Even though we had lived in the same house for seventeen years, she did not know where the bathrooms were, could not locate the light switches, and simply could not comprehend her surroundings.

CHAPTER 5

Memories of Happy Times

I do not wish to imply that happy times were absent. We had laughs, smiles, lots of hugs, and fun working in our flower garden. Although I did the work, Jo enjoyed being in the yard, and I guess she felt that she was helping. It was a pleasure to see her relatively calm during those times, even for short periods. As stated earlier, she had to be on the move so we walked around the yard often. We also took long walks around the neighborhood, sometimes a mile or so. She never seemed to tire. I would recommend to any other caregiver that they utilize walk-a-rounds as much as possible.

I recall one day that was especially memorable, at least for me. I had planted about a hundred tulip bulbs. They had bloomed in a glorious blaze of color and were just beautiful. Jo was happy walking around exploring her own yard and seemed quite content. I left her for a while in the rear yard to mow the front lawn; it did not take me more than ten or fifteen minutes. When I went back to check on her, she was still happy and seemed very serene. She came up to me giggling like a little child and gave me a tulip that she had picked. I immediately noticed over half of the other flowers were also uprooted. I took the flower, thanked her, kissed her on the forehead, and gave her a big hug. She squeezed me tightly and then gave me one of the sweetest smiles that I had not seen in a long time. It was very touching, but at the same time it almost yanked my heart out.

I have made several references to loss of communication; sometimes I felt so alone because of that. We had always been good, clear communicators; but as time took its continuing grip, Jo's ability to talk declined to basic confabulation (the making up of words), which came across as gibberish. It was difficult to interpret her speech earlier, but during the 1986-1988 period, it became more and more unintelligible. It did little good to ask her to repeat anything because I believe that she had already forgotten what she had said. As might be expected, that seemed to antagonize her and make her even more frustrated and difficult to deal with. Sometimes, I wondered who was the most frustrated.

I have mentioned hugging often. There is a good reason, I think, to place strong emphasis on that; it is necessary for *both* the patient and the caregiver. Often we hear about the victim of Alzheimer's or any other devastating life-robbing disease for that matter. We rarely hear of labeling the caregiver as a "victim." I submit that he/she is certainly a victim, more often than not a prisoner in a continuing hell. That is not meant to sound self-serving or designed to solicit any bravados. It is only an attempt to let those who are caregivers (be it for a spouse, mother, father, or other loved one) know that I admire them. I know, I have been there—I understand. Also, it is an attempt to educate those who may not know very much about this horrifying disease. Let the record show, I sincerely respect and admire any caregiver, particularly if it involves an Alzheimer victim. It is a victim-victim situation! Your friends and family must recognize that.

Speaking of friends—if you are just embarking on this long rough road, you will probably be shocked how some of your longtime friends will abandon you just when you need them the most. They may stop coming around or calling. Maybe it is because they cannot cope with the problem? Perhaps they do not know what to say or do? But do not be too surprised if that happens. You will weather the storm.

CHAPTER 6

Early Indicators

Many have asked, "What were the earliest symptoms observed in Jo with the onset of Alzheimer's disease?" As stated earlier, there were signs of things going wrong, but it is difficult to label them as "earliest symptoms"; many of which I did not recognize until after I had read many research papers and associated articles on the disease. Even then, I attempted to thread various events of her behavior to what I could piece together based on conversations with our family doctor, plus all the reading materials that I had collected. It should be noted that all my comments, recollections, ideas, and memories are obviously based on my personal experiences and exposure to Jo's illness. They may or may not be useful to the potential caregiver reader and should be viewed strictly as *my* experience and how I coped with those events.

At the risk of being repetitive, I must emphasize one cannot pinpoint to a specific onset of the horrible nightmare of Alzheimer's. After discussions with other family members and reviewing what we all remember, we believe Jo's illness started about 1980 at the age of forty-nine or fifty.

Early indicators included unexplained episodes of crying, interspersed with anger and frustration. That is understandable since we think that she knew something was going on, probably before anyone else did. She did not understand, nor did we, that an illness that none of us knew anything about was about to descend on our family. In retrospect, I think that bothered her more than we will ever know. Other things were evident too; she could not balance her checkbook, and she had no concept of simple math, even though she had competently worked for a major corporation as a bookkeeper. She had always handled our family finances and never had any problem balancing our checkbook; she could not even begin to do that now. Early on she began to ask repeatedly about the time. She had a watch, but seemed oblivious to it or what it was for. Often she questioned "What time is it?" four or five times in a span of ten minutes. Jo was terrified at the sound of splashing or running water, i.e., the flush of a toilet or running water in the kitchen sink. She would scream and run away from the sound. Needless to say, bathing became a big problem. I had to have help to get that done. Showers were okay in the early stages, but became impossible due to her screaming, rowdiness, and defensive biting. We later graduated to the bathtub, but I needed a nurse or another attendant to manage. Our bathroom always looked like a cyclone had hit it after Jo's bath.

It is time, I think, to mention once again the disjointed aspect of this story. It is not intentional or planned, although continuity is an important ingredient to a meaningful account of our story. I cannot help but recall our lives were also disjointed, uprooted, chaotic, and difficult. You will forgive me as I jump from one subject to another, but I am hopeful all future caregivers will appreciate and learn how to cope in a disjointed environment. It will be a truly different world. Do not worry, you will adapt; you have to! You will do things your way; devise new ways to accomplish yours, as well as your loved one's, goals. I hasten to add, be prepared to change or alter those goals. I realize that many caregivers' handbooks advise to do everything in "a routine manner" in order not to confuse the Alzheimer's patient. My goodness, in the middle and later stages of the disease, the patient is already incredibly confused and could care less if his/her day is "routine."

As already mentioned, you must adapt to a given situation to achieve an objective, whether it is bathing, getting dressed, ready for bed, eating, or preparing for a walk or outing. You will learn what works best for you and your loved one.

CHAPTER 7

Key Words

Believe me, tremendous amounts of energy are required to provide loving and protective care for your loved one. Sometimes, a well thought-out shortcut is worthwhile to get a task done in a way beneficial to all parties. You will learn what works best. Again, remember that you must *alter* and *adapt*.

If I could select one word as most important when caring for an Alzheimer's patient, it would have to be *patience*. Without a doubt, your patience will be tried time and again. Often anger will try to surface; but through your compassion, understanding, and love, patience will be the common denominator that will identify you as a caring caregiver.

On a regular basis, you will be faced with restlessness, agitation, striking out, and sometimes-violent outbursts; all common behaviors in Alzheimer's patients. Remember, each and every case is individual and special. You must be the one in control! It is up to *you* to find out what works best for your situation.

Instant Recall: it does not exist in all Alzheimer's patients. Oh, maybe in the early stages there is still some cognitive function; but generally, *recall* is a thing of the past. Being unable to think, to apply logic, to reason, or to perform simple tasks are things that trigger such frustration and tears in both the patient and the caregiver. The person providing the care, love, and protection must be in control; be as calm as possible and apply the "Serenity Prayer" daily.

God, grant me the serenity to accept the things I cannot change, the courage to change the things I can change and the wisdom to know the difference.

The person that you are caring for no longer has that wisdom; it is not their fault nor is it yours. Preillness conditions will be only a memory of yours. The Alzheimer's patient will, at times, exhibit flashes of brilliance by remembering events and things of fifty years ago with astonishing clarity, but will not know you or your name. Heartbreaking, but you will adapt to those conditions. Give them a hug or a smile and remember the Serenity Prayer. Inject humor into your daily activities. Cultivate humor into your thinking. It has a calming effect on all parties. Sometimes funny events occur that you will not forget. Funny may be the wrong word because it is so sad. Just before I retired in 1983 (to devote all of my time caring for Jo), I came in from work and found the iron in the refrigerator. It is descriptive in vivid detail of the Alzheimer patient's brain—it ceases to work at times. I knew that day what I had to do and took immediate steps to retire and become the caregiver. I could not visualize any other option. Our lives rapidly changed.

My thoughts often drifted back to earlier and happier times. I was grateful for the "good life" and wonderful travel experience that we had enjoyed. We had journeyed to Europe several times, the Mideast, Asia, and just about all of the United States. We were thankful for those opportunities. But now, I accepted the fact that they were over. Now, we were traveling a far different road. I had no idea how long or how bumpy it would become.

Another major recall event: one, which I will always remember, was when Jo woke up and looked at me and said, "Who are you? Get out of my bed." That was hard to take. It felt like a dull knife right in the heart. I knew that she was fading away at a much more rapid pace. She did not know me and, to be truthful, I did not know her now.

CHAPTER 8

Support Groups

By all means, I strongly recommend to associate yourself with a local Alzheimer's support group. It is an invaluable experience and will help you in multiple ways. You will be talking with and learning from people just like you. They have "been there, done that," and more likely they are there (just like you) ready to share experiences. You will learn from each other how to deal with stress, frustration, and heartaches because everyone is in the same boat. Remember a tide of camaraderie and mutual helpfulness raises all boats. This will prove to be one of the most important steps that you can take to help yourself. There you will find love, understanding, compassion, and caring people who help each other. It will be true support for what you are going through. It is a long trip—do not go alone!

I have attempted to include several articles that I think will assist most Alzheimer's caregivers. I have given credit to their authors in each instance (when known). I wish all could be identified, but some must remain anonymous simply because I cannot find out who they are. Bless them, for I believe that they would be pleased that their well-written thoughts might help someone else.

The No-Cost Way to Feel Better
(Support Groups)

If you've never been to a support group, you wonder what happens, what good will it do, will it just be sharing of sadness. You wonder if you can talk to strangers about your situation.

Coping with the day-to-day problems and physical care of a person with Alzheimer's is both emotionally and physically draining. It is different from any other illness. Because the disease causes personality and behavioral changes in your loved one, you may find yourself feeling embarrassed, impatient, exhausted and even angry. We are left feeling that no one can understand what happens in our daily lives or the frustration that we feel.

Something good happens when people who share similar situations get together in a Support Group. You must have a lot of questions . . . you may want more information. Since everyone in the group has "been there" or "is there" now, there is a sense of trust and understanding. You can believe and learn from others. You will experience that magic sense of relief that comes with knowing your problems and emotions are not so different and that you are not alone in your caregiving.

Both family members and caregivers of AD persons can benefit greatly from our free support groups. These groups are located throughout the country.

CHAPTER 9

Food for Thought

Excerpts from Various Alzheimer's Chapter Newsletters
St. Louis, Missouri Chapter
ADRDA
and Other Individuals

Those who suffer from dementia do live one day at a time; indeed, they are all fated to live in the eternal present. It is truly worth the effort to make each moment pleasant and meaningful for them. There is small profit in agonizing over yesterday's mistakes and failures. The person with dementia of the Alzheimer's type has the good fortune not to remember.

Tomorrow is forever shut off from the Alzheimer person, thank God. Tomorrow is forever there, however, for the caregiver and is only shut out with the greatest difficulty. Plan, yes, but the words are "Don't waste your time with futile fears and morbid musings."

We are all aware that long after dementia patients can no longer respond cognitively, they can, and do, respond emotionally. Fear and foreboding become tangible sensations resulting in disturbed patients and burned-out caregivers—definitely a no-win situation.

Admittedly, Alzheimer's disease is a no-win affliction of challenging dimensions. Life is the way it is, not the way it's supposed to be, and it is the way one copes with it that makes the difference acceptable. Each day can be a small victory. Look well, therefore, to this day.

Agitation at Sundown—Suggestions on How to Avoid It

1. Plan activities of the day so that there is less to do in late afternoon.
2. Schedule appointments and trips for the earlier part of the day.
3. Play quiet music instead of loud TV in the late afternoon.
4. Try to remember that the patient does not have control over his behavior; his annoying behavior is the inability of his brain to sort out a confusing environment.
5. Try to make the patient feel secure and well protected.
6. Do not argue with the patient.
7. Do not ask the patient to explain what is bothering him; he doesn't know, and he can't tell you.
8. Be sure the patient is getting enough exercise during the day.
9. If the patient is restless, try to get him interested in some quiet activity, such as folding towels. You will probably have to re-fold them, but that is okay.

—from How to Care for the Alzheimer's Patient,
Foundation for Hospice and Homecare,
via the Tucson, Arizona, Chapter Newsletter.

The Battle of the Bath

Some persons with dementing illness lose the desire to bath and change clothing, or may become upset and agitated when confronted with bath time. The process of undressing and getting into the tub or shower may make them feel vulnerable and at risk. Also, the process itself may be overwhelming, leading to increased fear, agitation, and resistance. While each individual with an Alzheimer-like disorder is unique, here are some general practices which a caregiver can usually adapt to specific situations.

Evaluate the best time for bathing. Do not schedule the bath or shower at times that are already stressful for you or your family member. Instead, select a time when you are least likely to have interruptions. Leaving a confused or physically frail person alone in a tub or shower could pose a real or imagined danger to the patient.

Frequency of bathing can also be evaluated. Persons who are elderly and not incontinent may not need a complete daily bath. A partial sponge bath alternated with more complete bath every two days may suffice.

Break the bathing process into small steps to avoid overwhelming your family member with too many instructions and demands. Make the routine as calm and non-threatening as possible, guiding and assisting them one small step at a time. Remember too, that the patient may have an altered sense of hot and cold. Adjust the water temperature to the patient's comfort, not necessarily to your own.

There are many ways to bath: showers, tub baths, sponge baths, or hand-held showers. Find which works best for both of you, and then maintain that routine for as long as it works well.

Assess for safety. This may mean adapting your bathroom facilities. Consider safety strips or bath mats that secure firmly to the tub surface. Grab bars and shower stools may be helpful accessories. These items are available at local medical supply houses or through the home care catalogues.

—from Temple, Texas
ADRDA Support Group Newsletter

"Combativeness"—A Behavior Problem

Common Behaviors in Alzheimer's Patients by Gerald Moriarty, MD (Edited, Sharon Lenhardt)

Restlessness—agitation—striking out. Outbursts such as these are usually brief, although at the time I'm sure it doesn't seem that way. Unfortunately this type of behavior is sometimes a distressing consequence of Alzheimer's Disease and a difficult problem to deal with. Where do you begin? The most important rule to remember—although it's easier said than done—is to *remain calm and in control*!!! Try to determine the cause, if possible; has frustration over something caused the outburst? If so, what's causing the frustration? Has there been a change in the environment? Furniture moved around? Has there been a change in daily routine? Is the patient physically uncomfortable for any reason? What is he/she trying to communicate to you? These are just a few superficial suggestions. It's up to you to discover, if possible, the cause, and find a feasible solution.

I can't stress "routine" enough: You must understand that it's impossible for an Alzheimer's victim to cope with reality, as we know it in everyday life. It's up to you to control this for him/her. "Diversion" can be a useful tool if you anticipate agitation. Divert his/her attention to something simple to comprehend: a bird outside the window; a song on the radio; a short walk; reinforce his/her sense of security; a touch of the hand may do the trick.

It sounds like a lot of work, doesn't it? It is! Again, the important thing is for you to remain in control! Yes, there are some situations that are impossible, where outbursts are frequent and/or intolerable. Medication may be the answer; however, be aware of any adverse side effects. Check with your physician and follow his recommendations.

Put yourself in the Alzheimer victim's shoes for a moment. Imagine how frustrating it must be to be locked in a world of confusion! How might you react? What would make your confused world a little easier to cope with? Yes, *it is* a lot of work—day in, and day out—but once you get the hang of it, you'll be able to cope better. Make sure you allow yourself some "free time"—get away on a regular basis. Set up a schedule for yourself. Hire a "sitter" who understands the situation and can handle it. Leave emergency contacts or a phone number where you can be reached.

Each and every case is individual and special. It's up to you to find what works best for your situation. To recap:

a) Try to anticipate situations which experience has shown are likely to provoke agitation.
b) REMAIN CALM!
c) Provide the patient with *simple*, clear explanations of what's happening. It may be obvious to you, but confusing, frightening, or frustrating to the patient.
d) Diversion—useful alternative.
e) Provide him/her with support and a sense of security.
f) ADRDA is just a call away—CALL US!

—from ADRDA Cincinnati

Caregiver's Feelings

Caring for a loved one with Alzheimer's is probably the most time consuming, stressful and thankless job imaginable. The tension and strain of being constantly alert and heedful to an AD patient leaves primary caregivers exhausted and with little time for themselves. We have all resented the lack of gratitude shown from the love one we care for so faithfully. Our patience wears thin when we must repeat and repeat and repeat any directive given to them as they stare into an unknown world from which we are excluded. Their failure to recognize us—we who spend so much time and energy bathing, dressing and feeding our loved ones—brings on hurt and anger.

How cruel a disease that allows a parent to forget a child, or a husband or wife to forget their spouse. This perhaps is the cruelest of all. So anger builds! We raise our voices to scold them, then feel guilty and cry. And it is alright to cry. These are normal feelings. Releasing our anger by crying is good. It is a healthy way to bring relief to the stress and anxiety we experience.

And which of us needs to be told that the financial burden is devastating? Sitters, homecare, special equipment for safety and comfort, or nursing home costs are overwhelming. Because of these expenses, we do without those things for which we have worked and saved.

As friends feel uncomfortable in the presence of an AD patient, their visits become less frequent. Family members offer little help in caring for the patient, while we are in desperate need of respite. We become isolated, depressed and bitter. We begin to question, "Why me? Why me?" So, we resent the patient until we realize we are really resenting the disease.

Yet, we are doing our best to cope in this "private hell" of Alzheimer's Disease. Who else but an Alzheimer's caregiver continues to love, sacrifice and stand by a loved one so unselfishly. Simply put, we are special people.

—June Calcagno

Laughter: A Therapeutic Experience
for Patient and Caregiver

In addition to the joy that **laughter** gives to the Alzheimer's patient, it often produces distinct, beneficial changes in their behavior. The most frequent change is an increase in alertness you can see when they understand a bit of humor. Much to the delight of caregivers, humor provides glimpses of unrecognized abilities.

Humor can also be used to make specific changes in behavior. Although the Alzheimer's patient may forget the details of an event, they may remember how they felt about it. You, as a caregiver, can use that emotional memory to influence how they will act in the future.

It is not only the patient that benefits from **laughter**; caregivers have noted the following benefits from the use of humor with Alzheimer's patients:

   ... Relief from the psychological burdens of the caregiver role.
   ... Relieve the patient or loved one of embarrassment.
   ... A sense of caring and enjoyment is communicated through the use of
        private jokes with the patient or loved one.

Familiar events that happened many times tend to be remembered by the AD patient well into the middle stages of the disease. Proverbs and sayings, holiday rituals, traditions, and familiar activities of everyday life can provide much material suitable for a humorous treatment. Whether you are a home caregiver or work in an adult day care center or a long-term facility, you can find endless ways of using humor to make your days more enjoyable and to enhance the quality of life for your loved ones and patients. You must be willing to risk being slightly ridiculous and willing to fail once in awhile. Remember, sometimes the joke's on you.

(Courtesy Janett Adasiak, RN.
Edited from the SW Florida
Chapter 2/91)

Back to Basics with Garden Therapy

Garden therapy is simple to define: It is the growing of fruits, vegetables, flowers and herbs as a fun and therapeutic activity. There are many variations, though, that can be adjusted to your loved ones' needs and abilities, and the activity leaves much room for creativity.

Garden therapy is physically and emotionally beneficial to both the patient and the caregiver. The emotional benefits abound. First, planting seeds and successfully nurturing plants until they are full grown lends tremendous feelings of accomplishment, and a good opportunity for caregivers to lavish patients with praise.

How to Interpret Body Language

At certain stages almost all persons suffering with Alzheimer's Disease have difficulty communicating. Either they can't find the words they want to use or, later on, they are unable to speak in meaningful sentences. Speech, however, is not the only means of expression.

There are many kinds of "body language" which help us to communicate. (1) If a person cannot make his wishes known with his words, he may be frustrated and anxious and may move around a lot. He may make some kind of sign or signal in an attempt to convey a desire. Any concentrated attention to a certain part of him may be a sign that there is pain or soreness in that area. Scratching or pressing on some part of the body may signal a health problem about which the loved one is not able to speak. (2) A fragmented sentence or babbling may be an attempt to convey some thought or need. Eventually the person will lose the use of words and we must depend on facial expressions, tone of voice, and the look in his eyes. It's very lonesome to be lost in time and space and caregivers must pay close attention to the gestures and facial expressions. We should also be aware that OUR gestures, facial expressions, and tone of voice would be interpreted by our loved one. If we speak loudly, they may be frightened.

Perhaps the single most important tool we have is the sense of touch. People who are agitated will often respond to body contact; a hug, a handshake, or some neck massage. It lets them know you're there and you care.

(excerpts from article by Bill Wiley, Honolulu Chapter)

Don't Ignore Dementia Symptoms
by Teressa Nolin

In truth, our greatest fear is not of death, after all, but of lingering death.

We know we can cope, if we must, with the gradual loss of physical abilities, but who doesn't tremble at the prospect of losing their mind.

It is this fear of dementia, that awful leaking away of the wits, that becomes the cruelest of afflictions.

Millions of people a year will fear for their own minds or for the mental abilities of loved ones. Unfortunately, far too many of them will delay professional help, in many cases postponing their own relief from the symptoms of dementia and fear.

The Alzheimer's Disease and Related Disorders Association, Inc. defines dementia as the loss of intellectual abilities to the point of interfering with a person's ability to function. In varying degrees, dementia will affect the abilities to think, reason, remember and perform routine tasks. Judgment, mental reflexes, abstract thinking and mood may also be impaired.

Alzheimer's Disease, the most common of the dementing disorders—and probably the most feared—affects up to four million Americans. Unfortunately, diagnosis is difficult and the cure, as yet, remains unknown.

However, more than 60 other conditions also result in dementia, including nutritional deficiencies, depression, thyroid problems, stroke, Huntington's Disease, multi-infarct dementia, Parkinson's Disease, brain tumors, syphilis, circulatory disease and Creutzfeldt-Jakob Disease. For a number of these problems, treatments do exist. Research and a growing public awareness offer hope for even better treatments, diagnosis and ultimately cures.

Unfortunately, many people cry Alzheimer's Disease at the slightest decline in mental ability. Or worse, they deny the problem altogether.

"It's not a given that just because you turn 60 you have Alzheimer's Disease," notes Janice Young, Executive Director of Alzheimer's Association Austin Chapter.

Because many of the conditions, which produce symptoms similar to Alzheimer's Disease are treatable, it is important for people to recognize symptoms and seek medical help.

"The first thing I usually tell people is to get a thorough physical exam—from head to toe," says Young. "If nothing shows up that's causing symptoms, then a neurologist should be consulted."

Neurological/psychological testing usually includes a CAT scan and magnetic resonance imaging to determine problems in the brain, as well as specific areas of the brain affected. Examinations also should include a mental status test to evaluate orientation, attention, recent recall and the ability to calculate. This evaluation also will test the abilities to read, write, copy drawings, repeat, understand and make judgments.

Getting Help

If the individual showing symptoms is unable or unwilling to seek medical help, then family members should intervene.

The first step, advises Young, is to have a family meeting and decide a course of action. Many times, she admits, taking action can be emotionally trying for family members, particularly if some family members deny the problem.

"There are some family members who see it as plain as day, and others who refuse to accept the reality," she says. In any case, "There's not one way—it will be different for every family."

Many families will be forced to resort to subterfuge to get a loved one to a doctor, she admits.

"You might not necessarily want to tell the person a long time ahead that they're going to the doctor," says Young. If it has been a while since the patient has had a physical, you might simply encourage them to submit to a routine physical. But do alert the doctor in advance as to the real purpose of the visit.

"You don't ever want to confront the person with their deficits," she advises. Many times patients actually realize they are having problems and struggle desperately to keep the symptoms secret, Young explains. For resistant patients, the Alzheimer's Association recommends finding another "physical" reason for the patient to go to the doctor. For instance, suggest a check-up for a symptom that the patient is willing to acknowledge, such as eye problems, headaches, high blood pressure or the possibility of heart disease or diabetes.

Family members should be prepared to provide the doctor with as much specific information as possible, such as incidences illustrating a decrease in abilities, memory or personality changes. Observe and report what simple tasks now seem frustrating or impossible for the patient to perform, such as balancing a checkbook or using everyday tools.

Note how driving, personal habits, reading, writing and work performance have changed. Be sure to mention if a person seems unusually forgetful or gets lost in familiar surroundings.

Above all, try not to pre-diagnose. This is a difficult enough task for trained medical professionals. Your wrong assumptions can be very damaging, not only to your loved one, but also to your own peace of mind.

CHAPTER 10

Sharing Ways of Caring

Twelve Steps for Caregivers
by Carol J. Farran, DNSc, RN, and Eleanor Keane-Hagerty, MA

The Twelve Steps were originally developed as the heart of the Alcoholics Anonymous (AA) program to provide a unity of purpose and guidance for individual growth. Many professionals and self-help groups have adapted the twelve steps for various purposes.

The Twelve Steps focus on three different areas. First, they acknowledge that human resources such as intelligence, knowledge, strength, and hope are not enough to help people solve problems. Second, they explain the need to accept the help of a Higher Power to guide thoughts and actions. Finally, they suggest ways that the Power can be brought into one's daily life so that action can be taken.

In our research with caregivers of persons with dementia, one wife reported that she was applying the Twelve Steps to her caregiving experiences and challenged us to incorporate some of these ideas into our eight-week intervention program. We reviewed caregiver responses to our structured research interviews and noted additional comments frequently made by caregivers. From these comments we have compiled Twelve Steps for Caregivers.

Step 1: I can control how the disease affects me and my relatives. It is important for caregivers to understand that Alzheimer's Disease (AD) is a chronic and ultimately terminal disease. It is also important that caregivers realize which aspects of caregiving they can control, and acknowledge those aspects over which they have no control. Ultimately, no matter what the caregiver does, the disease process will not change. Caregivers can, however, learn to control such things as disruptive behaviors and their attitudes toward these behaviors. The AA Serenity Prayer has been helpful to many caregivers: "God, grant me the serenity to accept the things I cannot change, the courage to change the things I can change, and the wisdom to know the difference."

Step 2: I need to take care of myself. For most caregivers, this is a difficult lesson to learn. Some feel that they must always put other people first and that, it is selfish to think of doing things for themselves. They must learn that in order to continue providing care for their patients, they must first take care of themselves. Therefore, caregivers need to give themselves permission to obtain relief by using sources of respite and by involvement in outside activities they enjoy. For some caregivers, self-care becomes a real issue when they can no longer provide full-time care and must consider in-home assistance or nursing home placement. These decisions are difficult, since caregivers may feel that they are failures, are selfish, and are not keeping a promise made to the patient. Some caregivers need help to realize that the demands of providing care for a person with dementia may exceed individual resources. They need to see themselves as important and to acknowledge their abilities and preferences when making caregiving decisions.

Step 3: I need to simplify my lifestyle. It is essential that caregivers identify what is most important, what should be taken care of immediately, and what should receive most of their attention. As caregiving responsibilities take up more and more of their daily lives, other activities must be adapted or dropped. Caregivers will need to lower unrealistic expectations they may have of themselves.

Step 4: I need to allow others to help me. This step can be difficult for caregivers who have lived most of their lives thinking they "should" be independent and for those who view asking for help as a sign of weakness. Along with cultivating the gift of allowing others to help, they need to learn how to actively ask others for help. We encourage caregivers to keep a list of activities nearby, and when friends say, "Call me if you need help," the caregiver can easily refer to the list and ask for a specific kind of help. Too, presenting others with a variety of specific tasks allows time to volunteer real assistance.

Step 5: I need to take one day at a time. Borrowed directly from AA, this slogan commonly used by family caregivers reinforces the importance of thinking only about the day's challenges and helps caregivers focus their energies on what is most important in the short term. It also lessens feelings of being overwhelmed when looking ahead to concerns, which may never develop. For the person with dementia, it is essentially the "here and now" that is significant—a reality to which caregivers must adapt.

Step 6: I need to structure my day. Because of the memory impairment brought on by AD, it is important that the caregiver develop a sense of structure, routine, and rituals for their patient. This helps the patient to feel more safe and secure, and caregivers can use their time and energy more efficiently.

Step 7: I need to have a sense of humor. Caregivers often report that a sense of humor helps them through a difficult situation. One reported, "I choose to make this a humorous heartache." Another said, "You have to laugh. You can't cry all the time." Maintaining a sense of humor means caregivers must be objective and see the irony in painful situations.

Step 8: I need to remember that my patient's behavior and emotions are distorted by the illness. In our research, we found that while, in an intellectual way, caregivers generally understand dementia as a disease process, they are more likely to take it personally and feel that the patient is being difficult or getting back at them when disruptive behaviors occur. Caregivers need to attribute to the disease what rightfully belongs to the disease, and not simply to the relationship.

Step 9: I need to focus on and enjoy what my patient can still do. Caregivers frequently report that what helps them through the process of caregiving is to be able to see who their patient is in the present, as well as to appreciate what the person was in the past. Enjoying the good moments for what they provide is seen by caregivers as a way of helping themselves through the present difficulties. Focusing on what the person can still do also maintains patient independence and prevents "excess disability."

Step 10: I need to depend on other relationships for love and support. Caregivers often report that one of the most difficult aspects of caregiving is the loss of who this person once was. A daughter remarked, "We are losing my mother piece by piece." As this process continues, caregivers must increasingly look to other family members and friends for the love and support they once received from the impaired family member. Caregivers must understand that a desire to be cared about and supported by others is a normal human response and that it is essential to have these needs met in some way.

Step 11: I need to remind myself that I am doing the best I can at this very moment. Caregivers will not handle every situation perfectly, and at times they will become impatient and angry with the patient. They will always be able to see things they might have done differently or better. However, it is important for caregivers to acknowledge their human limitations, develop a sense of acceptance for themselves, and accept the way they managed a particular situation. Second-guessing and feelings of guilt are common with caregivers, but it is important for them to immerse themselves in positive reinforcement so that their precious time and energy are not siphoned off into self-defeating thoughts.

Set 12: A Higher Power is available to me. Many caregivers report their sense that a Higher Spiritual Power has assisted them through difficult situations. However, other caregivers strongly challenge the use of a Higher Power because of their own beliefs. We draw from AA and other approaches to say that we are not imposing a set of beliefs on other people, but that we do encourage caregivers to develop their own conception of this Higher Power and how this power might work in their own lives through the caregiving situation.

—Excerpted from the *American Journal of Alzheimer's Care and Related Disorders and Research*, November/December 1989

CHAPTER 11

Praying for Help

The Difference

I got up early one morning
and rushed right into the day;
I had so much to accomplish
that I didn't have time to pray.

Problems just tumbled about me
and heavier came each task;
"Why doesn't God help me?" I wondered.
He answered, "You didn't ask."

I wanted to see joy and beauty,
but the day toiled on, gray and bleak;
I wondered why God didn't show me.
He said, "But you didn't seek."

I tried to come into God's presence;
I used all my keys at the lock.
But, God gently and lovingly chided,
"My child, you didn't knock."

I woke up early this morning,
and paused before entering the day;
I had so much to accomplish that
I had to take time to pray.

Author unknown

CHAPTER 12

If I Had My Life to Live Over

I'd dare to make more mistakes next time. I'd relax, I'd limber up. I would be sillier than I have been this trip. I would take fewer things seriously. I would take more chances. I would climb more mountains and swim more rivers. I would eat more ice cream and less beans. I would perhaps have more actual troubles, but I'd have fewer imaginary ones.

You see, I'm one of those people who live sensibly and sanely hour after hour, day after day. Oh, I've had my moments, and if I had it to do over again, I'd have more of them. In fact, I'd try to have nothing else. Just moments, one after another, instead of living so many years ahead of each day. I've been one of those persons who never goes anywhere without a thermometer, a hot water bottle, a raincoat and a parachute. If I had to do it again, I would travel lighter than I have.

If I had my life to live over, I would start barefoot earlier in the spring and stay that way later in the fall. I would go to more dances. I would ride more merry-go-rounds. I would pick more daisies.

So, here's to life! (Don't forget to pick the daisies.)

Written by Nadine Stair when she was eighty-five years old

CHAPTER 13

Caregiving Tips

A round the house

- Cover all unused outlets with childproof plugs.
- Unplug all cords, install power switches, and remove knobs on major appliances if unsupervised attempts have been made to use the equipment.
- Keep all power tools and machinery locked in the garage, workroom, or basement.
- Remove all guns or other weapons from the house, or at least store guns unloaded in a locked cabinet. Be sure to store ammunition in a separate, secured location.
- Hide an extra key outside or leave one with a trusted neighbor. Patients can accidentally lock the caregiver out of the house.
- When doing the laundry at home for a nursing-home patient, give each article a tiny spray of cologne. Try to use a scent that has been a favorite of hers.
- Mirrors can sometimes frighten your patient, so you may want to turn them around, cover them, or remove them entirely.
- Instead of sewing nametags on the inside of the patient's clothing, consider sewing them on the outside. This way, the staff at the nursing home does not have to hunt for the owner of a piece of clothing. Those who have tried it find that clothes are lost less often. Also, the patient is more apt to be called by name.
- Using signs or symbols on bathroom doors have proven to be successful in one nursing home experiment. Incontinence was reduced by as much as 15 percent.

In the bathroom

- Turn down the temperature on the water heater to 120°F to avoid scalding. Always check the temperature of bath or shower water before use.
- Place nonskid adhesive strips, decals, or mats in shower or tub.
- Install grab bars in the tub or shower and beside toilet.
- Use contrasting colors for toilet seats, grab bars, and hot water taps to make them easier to see.
- Use night-lights in the bedroom, hallway, bathroom, and throughout the home.
- Use a plastic shower stool and a handheld showerhead to make bathing easier.
- Remove wastebaskets and any other receptacles that may be mistaken for a toilet.

For safety's sake

- Have emergency numbers and home addresses prominently displayed near all phones.
- Smoking, if permitted at all, should only be done under close supervision. Keep all matches, lighters, cigarettes, and ashtrays in a secured location.
- Install smoke alarms in the kitchen and sleeping areas. Check regularly to maintain proper working order. Obtain a fire extinguisher. Be sure to train household members in the use of this equipment.
- Remove all knives or other sharp items from the kitchen and elsewhere throughout the house.
- Remove clutter from all areas of home.
- Remove scatter or throw rugs. Replace or remove torn carpet.
- Store breakable or valuable items in a locked cabinet.
- Store all prescription medications, over-the-counter drugs, household cleaning compounds, laundry supplies, paint products and other poisons, such as insecticides and fertilizers out of reach or in a locked cupboard.

Take Care of Yourself!

The physical demands and emotional trauma of caring for a loved one whose mind is being destroyed by Alzheimer's can end up wrecking the caregiver's health too.

If you, or someone you know, is an AD caregiver, here are a few helpful hints:

- Don't expect to be appreciated. A caregiver's satisfaction should come from within. The victim is often not able to express gratitude. Remember, insults are not meant.
- It's okay to get angry. But use your anger constructively; don't vent it on the Alzheimer's victim. Scrub floors, chop wood, or just go outside and jump up and down. Let it out. You'll feel better.
- Develop a support system of friends or relatives with whom you can talk and share your feelings.
- Most of all, make time for yourself, no matter what it takes. Get someone, a friend or professional, to come in at least a few hours a week. Or find facilities in your community that provide day care or even short-term stays of a week or so.
- A little time off will make a world of difference in your outlook—and in your physical health.

A Caregiver Writes
Shattered Dreams

You dream of the day when you can retire
And do all the things that you desire
But just when you're getting ready to start
You get some news that just breaks your heart.
Your spouse was diagnosed—Alzheimer's Disease
Not him you say. Oh no, God, please!
Your plans and your life are suddenly changed
Everything you planned will have to be rearranged
You feel so helpless when you see your spouse
Can't find his way around his own house.
You show him pictures and his favorite chair
He doesn't remember that he lives there.
His eyes are dim and his walk is slow
We tell him we love him, we want him to know.
Our dreams of a future have been shattered.
But the loving and caring was all that mattered.
If you have a loved one or friend with this disease
Be kind, loving and understanding please.
Tell them you love them and hold their hand
And pray when you do they will understand.

—Frances Guisinger
Toledo, Ohio

CHAPTER 14

Communicating with the Alzheimer's Patient

Difficulty in communicating with others is a common problem associated with Alzheimer's disease (AD). In fact, it is usually one of the symptoms displayed during the early stages of the illness. The affected person may not be able to make himself (or herself—AD strikes men and women equally) understood or be able to understand what others are trying to say. Problems with communication may also result when the individual cannot organize thoughts into words or cannot express all of the words in a thought. If the Alzheimer's patient has been covering up problems with communication, he may become angry or defensive at times when he cannot find the words to respond to questions or comments. At times the patient may appear uncooperative when in fact he simply cannot understand what someone is trying to say.

If you are having problems communicating with an AD patient, first make sure that he is not suffering from a hearing impairment. Then, keep the following in mind: the AD patient may forget within seconds even the information he understood; he may be able to read, but may not be able to understand the thought behind what has been read; what may be understood if heard in person can be lost if told over the phone.

Early in the disease, communication may be helped by combined use of signs, labels or written messages, and verbal instructions. Especially at this time, it is important to assume that the person understands more than he can express. Never talk about the patient as if he were not there.

Helping an AD patient communicate takes patience and understanding. Some suggestions include: (1) show interest in what the person is trying to say or feeling being expressed; (2) pay attention to the person's voice and gestures for clues to what he is feeling, since sometimes the emotions are more important than the words; (3) if the person cannot find a word, offer a guess; (4) if you don't understand, let the person know and encourage him to point or gesture; and (5) be calm and supportive.

To help the AD patient understand what *you* are trying to say: (1) address the person by name to gain his attention; (2) keep noise and distraction to a minimum; (3) speak slowly, calmly, and distinctly; (4) use short, simple, familiar words and sentences; (5) ask one question at a time and give the person time to respond; (6) demonstrate your request by drawing, pointing at, or touching things; (7) use nonverbal communication (a smile or a hug) to reinforce verbal communication or to communicate when the person no longer understands words. When using nonverbal communication, remember to move slowly and touch gently; do not startle. A smile can give reassurance.

Always treat the Alzheimer's patient with dignity and respect; remember that he is an adult. It is often easy to "talk down" to someone because you are using simple words or sentences. Your observation and sensitivity to the nature of communication techniques will help you both understand the messages you are trying to convey.

CHAPTER 15

Caregivers Stress and Coping Study

The following information was obtained from the Alzheimer's Association in Chicago, Illinois. You should remember to call on them for updated materials concerning the disease itself, tips, hints to help, etc. They are experts and most willing to help the caregiver in so many ways.

They can be contacted via their Web site at www.alz.org, or call them toll free at 1-800/272-3900.

10 Symptoms of Caregiver Stress

1. Denial about the disease and its effects on the person who has been diagnosed. *I know Mom's going to get better.*
2. Anger at the person with Alzheimer's or others, anger that no cure exists, and anger that people don't understand what's going on. *If he asks me that question one more time, I'll scream.*
3. Social withdrawal from friends and activities that once brought pleasure. *I don't care about getting together with the neighbors anymore.*
4. Anxiety about facing another day and what the future holds. *What happens when he needs more care than I can provide?*
5. Depression that begins to break your spirit affects the ability to cope. *I don't care anymore.*
6. Exhaustion that makes it nearly impossible to complete necessary daily tasks. *I'm too tired for this.*

7. Sleeplessness caused by a never-ending list of concerns. *What if she wanders out of the house or falls and hurts herself?*
8. Irritability that leads to moodiness and triggers negative responses and reactions. *Leave me alone!*
9. Lack of concentration makes it difficult to perform familiar tasks. *I was so busy, I forgot we had an appointment.*
10. Health problems that begin to take their toll, both mentally and physically. *I can't remember the last time I felt good.*

Others Care Too

Attached is a self-explanatory letter from a group of researchers at the University of California, San Francisco.

I participated in their study on caregivers' stress and how they cope. It was an interesting experience, and I hope my input was helpful. Even after I moved to Texas in April 1990, they still called me regularly in their follow-up studies.

UNIVERSITY OF CALIFORNIA, SAN FRANCISCO

BERKELEY • DAVIS • IRVINE • LOS ANGELES • RIVERSIDE • SAN DIEGO • SAN FRANCISCO   SANTA BARBARA • SANTA CRUZ

HUMAN DEVELOPMENT & AGING PROGRAM   1350 - 7th Avenue, CSBS 237
CENTER FOR SOCIAL & BEHAVIORAL SCIENCES   San Francisco. CA 94143-0848
                                                                     (415) 476-7285

October 16, 1989

Mr. Bill Smith
38245 Kimbro St
Fremont, CA 94536

Dear Mr. Smith,

You'll remember that about a year ago you were interviewed as part
of a study of people taking care of a close relative with Alzheimer's
Disease or a similar problem. At that time, an interviewer talked
with you about your experiences as a caregiver: for example, you
were asked about the energy which caregiving takes, the things you've
learned, the ways you deal with the situation, and your health and
well-being.

We're writing to thank you for your past participation, as well as
to let you know that we are entering the next phase of our work. As
we promised last year, we shall soon be contacting you again, hoping
to learn about how you've gotten along in the past year, and
especially about the changes you've experienced since the last
interview.

This research, funded by the U.S. Public Health Service, is probably
the largest and most comprehensive study of caregivers in the
country. Your cooperation was enormously helpful to the aims of the
study and we appreciate the time you spent with us, time spent away
from your already busy life. We're now in the process of analyzing
the information from the first set of interviews, and we shall soon
be writing papers describing what we've learned from these important
interviews. In the meantime, we've enclosed a page with a few of the
preliminary results from the research.

We still have much to learn from you. In the next weeks, an
interviewer will call to schedule an interview for a time that is
convenient for you.

Please accept our sincere thanks both for your past help and for your
future participation in this important research.

Sincerely,

Leonard I. Pearlin

Leonard I. Pearlin, Ph.D.
Professor and Principal Investigator
Caregivers Stress and Coping Study

University of California, San Francisco
Caregivers Stress and Coping Study

Here are a few of the very early results from the study. Each person we talked to had a unique set of answers to the many questions we asked, but we can report some general trends. All in all, we talked to 555 caregivers, 300 in the Bay Area and 255 in Los Angeles. The study is limited to husbands and wives, and sons and daughters of patients, including sons—and daughters-in-law. The participants in the study were actively involved in caregiving for periods ranging from just a few months to more than 11 years.

- Caregivers first noticed that something was wrong about three years before their relatives needed to be cared for.
- Memory loss and personality changes were the two most commonly reported problems, which first made caregivers realize something was wrong.
- Caregivers report a sense of loss associated with the illness: they feel that they are losing or have lost the person they used to confide in, and that they have lost the ability to plan for the future with confidence.
- "Overloaded" is a common feeling among family members: about half of the caregivers report going to bed completely exhausted, or close to it.
- Despite the pressures and strains, many family members report rewards from caregiving, most often involving the development of themselves as stronger and wiser people.
- More than three quarters of the caregivers regularly use some formal services, most often adult day care, support groups, or an attendant.
- Although caregivers often do not have much time for social activities, many feel supported by their friends and families.
- Caregivers try to develop ways of coping with caregiving demands, often by trying to keep their sense of humor or by simply not looking too far into the future.
- Caregiving can take its toll on the health of family members: more than one-third of the caregivers felt that their own health had deteriorated since they had begun looking after their relative.
- Despite this toll, more than three quarters still felt that they were in good health.

These are but a few of the preliminary findings. As the study goes on, we shall be learning much more about the problems of caregivers, how they try to deal with those problems as the circumstances of their lives change, and the long-term effects of caregiving on health and well-being.

Ways to Reduce Caregiver Stress

- Know what resources are available in your community.
- Become educated about Alzheimer's disease and caregiving techniques.
- Get help from family, friends and community resources.
- Take care of yourself by watching your diet, exercising and getting plenty of rest.
- Manage your level of stress by consulting a physician and using relaxation techniques.
- Accept changes as they occur.
- Engage in legal and financial planning.
- Be realistic about what you can do.
- Give yourself credit for what you have accomplished; don't feel guilty if you lose patience or can't do everything on your own.

Understanding the reality. Alzheimer's disease is:

- a physical disease that destroys
- not a normal part of aging
- not limited to the elderly
- not currently curable, but help for body functions, not just memory is available

Note: The association's motto says it well—The Compassion to Care, the Leadership to Conquer

CHAPTER 16

Things to Do/Visiting Others

Things You Must Do

Decisions you must make now should be a top priority—but use the advice of a good lawyer. One of the more important decisions is to get a power of attorney, which will enable you to handle all financial considerations concerning assets, real estate transactions, etc. Another important step is to obtain a power of attorney for health care and medical decisions.

A competent attorney can advise you on steps to take to protect your assets and investments, as well as those of the Alzheimer's patient.

Obviously, I am not legally trained, nor do I profess to offer legal advice; but I do know *you* should take the critical steps suggested above. They will prove to be important.

Visiting Friends

Many times, especially when the caregiver is really tired and exhausted (lack of sleep, stress, etc.), an outing of any kind is a welcome break for him/her. Some degree of planning before embarking on an "outside" visit is strongly recommended. The preparation should include:

1. Take the patient to the bathroom.
2. Usually after a bathing session is best.

3. Feed your patient a meal—or utilize some small snack.
4. Include the patient in planning to "go out." (They love to be "on the move.")
5. Be prepared for the unthinkable!

That last item deserves explanation. Actually, I could have inserted this on the segment of HUMOR—but I just remembered it. I guess that is evidence of my disjointed approach to this journal.

Now, for the explanation: We decided to visit some dear friends (after warning them in advance we were coming). Everything was going well—Jo was happy and manageable. She *sat* in the floor playing with some paper dolls and real dolls, which belonged to our friends' granddaughter. Suddenly, Jo indicated she had to go to the bathroom by making certain gestures (rubbing and touching herself). Always alert to these clues, I promptly escorted her to the restroom. After "arranging" her for the event, I briefly left her there and went back to our friends' den. A few minutes passed—long enough for me to realize that she may need assistance. I went back to see about her. I saw her all right—all of her. She was skipping down the hall toward the den—stark naked! These episodes of "inappropriate behavior" did not happen too often, but they did occur. On occasion, she would spew forth-outrageous profanity, which she *never* uttered before her illness.

You learn, sometimes the hard way, to cope with almost any situation. Sometimes you laugh—other times you cry. Often I would say to myself, thank goodness for the humor even if it's sad.

CHAPTER 17

Time to Make a Change

It's Time for Action

In mid-1989, I did what I said would never happen. At the insistence and prodding of our family doctor, I placed Jo in a nursing facility. He told me my health and well-being "was going down the drain" and he had made arrangements for Jo to enter a nursing home for better and more professional around-the-clock care. I wanted desperately to avoid that, but after family discussions and operating on our doctor's reasoning, it was decided to be the most prudent action.

About a year later, after analyzing my financial condition, I decided to move Jo (to a much less expensive area in Texas) as it was costing over $150 per day—every day—for her care in California. That was the cost then, back in the '80s. I'm confident that it is much more today. The costs were much lower in Texas, although they would rise even higher as time went by. Of course, I do not regret a dime—it was okay as long as Jo received good care. Thank goodness we had saved enough to be able to pay for her care.

Nursing Home Care
(Is It a Viable Option?)

There are specialized care options available—in-home care, nursing homes (some with special Alzheimer's "wings"), in-home nursing care, etc. Some of these choices can be very expensive, so you must weigh all options according to your means.

Family discussions can often contribute various ideas on what to do and how to do it. A family consensus is generally helpful to everyone involved. Your family doctor's advice can help in these major decisions, as well as advice and counsel of your clergy.

CHAPTER 18

Confession Time—An Update

In the beginning,
The word was chocolate
And it was good.

—Anonymous

S ometimes good things are obvious.

My experiences as a caregiver were challenging, heavy laden, memorable, and provided me with firsthand insight on life and its associated burdens. But there were good things too, which defined me as a man, husband, and father as well as my overall character.

I'm proud of what I did—I don't regret one minute!

Regarding the "confessional" alluded to above, I wish to bring this story up to date. It was started so many years ago, 1991 to be exact. I have tried, as best I can, to accurately record the events as they happened. I have forgotten some because I don't want to remember them—perhaps because they are too hard and too personal to report.

Fast forward, if you will, to 2006. Of course, much has changed. Don is now fifty-six, Glen is fifty-four, my granddaughter Heather is thirty-three and now married, Holly is thirty-one, and Stephanie is twenty-one and a senior at San Diego State.

Jo would have been so proud **to see** all "the kids," but it wasn't meant to be. Alzheimer's disease took its cruel course and Jo's life in October 1994. After reconstructing all of those memories of that thirteen-and-a-half-year journey as caregiver, I've decided it was a valued and memorable experience. As for me, I'm now seventy-eight years old and was fortunate to find a wonderful mate. I found my "high school sweetheart," a girl that I had known for over sixty years. We were married about ten years ago. So it proves the dark clouds of your life can, and do, emerge with happiness and a silver lining. I'm grateful for that.

After a lot of soul searching and serious thought upon Jo's death, my boys and I discussed, in detail, what good could come of her passing. We mutually agreed to have a complete autopsy and donate Jo's brain to Alzheimer's research. These procedures were done at Scott & White Memorial Hospital in Temple, Texas. Our reasons were obvious—maybe, just maybe, someone else could be helped to avoid or treat this horrible disease—maybe even us!

More likely than not, the reader of this story will be an Alzheimer's caregiver. That thought gives me another opportunity to say, "May God bless you and know what sincere admiration I have for you and your noble efforts."

CHAPTER 19

Conclusion

Looking back on this journey, I have tried to reconcile events as they happened; admittedly as I've explained, sometimes out of sequence. But hopefully, those who find themselves in a similar role will more readily understand why my story is disjointed than one who hasn't experienced the nightmare of Alzheimer's firsthand.

Several have asked me, "How did you do it? What did you do to cope with it for so long? How did your family deal with it?" (And a dozen other questions, I might add.) Some of these questions I have already answered—others defy a clear response. I often wondered if my expanded family *really* understood what was going on with Jo, my immediate family, and me. Of course, their concern and compassion was very evident, but there were times when I felt "something" was missing. I don't have a clue as to what that "something" was. I never allowed myself to dwell on it. I came to the conclusion it was best to dismiss it from my mind.

One final thought—once again, may I express my sincere admiration to all caregivers—especially those involved with an Alzheimer's patient. You will be rewarded in untold ways. May God bless you and your noble efforts. I know that is a repeat thought, but it is worth repeating.

Good luck!

Note: I hope you live to be 120—and the last voice you hear is mine!